The Science of
a Pair of Glasses

The Science of Light

By Brian Williams

Science and Curriculum Consultant:
Debra Voege, M.A., *Science Curriculum Resource Teacher*

Gareth Stevens
Publishing

Please visit our web site at **www.garethstevens.com**.

For a free color catalog describing Gareth Stevens Publishing's list of high-quality books, call 1-800-542-2595 (USA) or 1-800-387-3178 (Canada). Gareth Stevens Publishing's fax: 1-877-542-2596

Library of Congress Cataloging-in-Publication Data

Williams, Brian, 1943–

    The science of a pair of glasses / by Brian Williams ; science and curriculum consultant, Debra Voege.

        p. cm. — (The science of—)

    Includes bibliographical references and index.

    ISBN-10: 1-4339-0044-0   ISBN-13: 978-1-4339-0044-0 (lib. bdg.)

    1. Optics—Juvenile literature.   2. Lenses—Juvenile literature.

    3. Eyeglasses—Juvenile literature. I. Title.

    QC360.W55   2009

    535—dc22   2008038767

This North American edition first published in 2009 by

Gareth Stevens Publishing

A Weekly Reader® Company

1 Reader's Digest Road

Pleasantville, NY 10570-7000 USA

This U.S. edition copyright © 2009 by Gareth Stevens, Inc.

Original edition copyright © 2008 by Franklin Watts. First published in Great Britain in 2008 by Franklin Watts, 338 Euston Road, London NW1 3BH, United Kingdom.

For Discovery Books Limited:

Editor: Rebecca Hunter   Designer: Keith Williams

Illustrator: Stefan Chabluk   Photo researcher: Rachel Tisdale

Gareth Stevens Executive Managing Editor: Lisa M. Herrington

Gareth Stevens Senior Editor: Barbara Bakowski

Gareth Stevens Creative Director: Lisa Donovan

Gareth Stevens Cover Designer: Keith Plechaty

Gareth Stevens Electronic Production Manager: Paul Bodley

Gareth Stevens Publisher: Keith Garton

Special thanks to Laura Anastasia, Michelle Castro, and Jennifer Ryder-Talbot

Photo credits: Shutterstock, cover; istockphoto.com/Jane Norton, p. 4; istockphoto.com/Ben Blankenburg, p. 5; istockphoto.com/Sunagotov Dmitry, p. 6; Getty Images/Charles Gupton/ Stone, p. 9; istockphoto.com/ Rui Matos, p. 11; Corbis, p. 13; istockphoto.com, p. 14; Getty Images/Hulton Archive, p. 15; Corbis/ Michael A. Keller, p. 16; istockphoto.com/Jodie Coston, p. 18; Corbis/Jim Craigmyle, p. 19; istockphoto.com/ Liza McCorkle, p. 20; Corbis/Charles Gupton, p. 21; Corbis/Hulton-Deutsch Collection, p. 22; Shutterstock, p. 23 top; Corbis/Alan Schein Photography, p. 23 bottom; istockphoto.com/Marcin Stalmach, p. 24; Corbis/Steve Marcus/Reuters, p. 25; istockphoto.com, p. 26 & 27 top; Corbis/Roger Ressmeyer, p. 27 bottom; Getty Images/David Deas/DK Stock, p. 28; Getty Images/National Geographic, p. 29 top; istockphoto.com, p. 29 bottom. Every effort has been made to trace copyright holders. We apologize for any inadvertent omissions and would be pleased to insert appropriate acknowledgments in a subsequent edition.

Printed in the United States of America

1 2 3 4 5 6 7 8 9 10 09 08

Contents

Words that appear in **boldface** type are in the glossary on page 30.

The Eyes Have It

Glasses can improve your view of the world! Some people need eyeglasses to read more easily and see objects more clearly. How do glasses help? It's all about light and **lenses**.

What Goes Into Glasses?

Glasses look simple—two pieces of glass or clear plastic set in a frame. Each piece of glass or plastic is a lens. The frame has two arms, called temples. The arms have hinges so that the glasses can be folded and placed in a case. A central bridge with pads grips the nose lightly.

▼ *The main parts of a pair of eyeglasses are the frame and the lenses.*

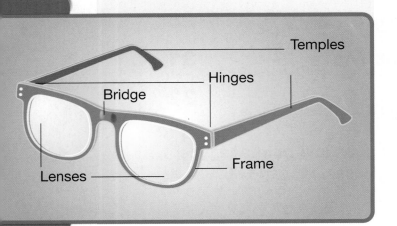

Temples

Hinges

Bridge

Frame

Lenses

Who Wears Eyewear?

Although eyesight usually worsens as people grow older, some kids need glasses. Studies show that about one in four children wears glasses or other corrective lenses. Girls are more likely than boys to wear glasses or lenses.

▲ *Wearing glasses helps many people read more easily.*

▲ *These skiers wear sunglasses to protect their eyes from the bright **glare** of sunlight on snow.*

Some children have a vision screening test at school. Others are tested during a medical checkup. If a vision problem is found, an eye care specialist checks each eye. He or she then writes a **prescription** for corrective lenses to be fitted into a frame.

Sun and Safety

People also wear glasses to protect their eyes. Sunglasses filter out bright sunshine and the glare from snow. Safety glasses, goggles, and visors shield eyes from damage at work or play. Eye protection is important when handling chemicals, cutting metal, skiing, or riding a motorcycle.

Seeing the Light

No light, no sight! Light, reflected from objects to our eyes, enables us to see. Light is a form of **energy** from the Sun and other stars. All light comes from tiny particles called **atoms** giving off energy. The atoms can be in anything from the Sun to a lightbulb.

Lit by Nature

Natural light comes from the Sun, other stars, or creatures such as fireflies. People cannot control natural light. Artificial light comes from a source such as an electric lamp or a candle. Artificial light can be controlled.

Lines of Light

Light travels as **rays**, made up of tiny particles called **photons**. The rays travel in straight lines. You can test this by shining a flashlight into a dark room. The light beam seems to hit the wall instantly. The speed of light is 186,000 miles (300,000 kilometers) per second.

NEVER look directly at the Sun. It is so bright, it can damage your eyes.

Breaking Through

Different materials let different amounts of light pass through. **Transparent**, or see-through, glass lets light rays pass

◄ *The Sun is a star, a ball of very hot gas that gives off light.*

6

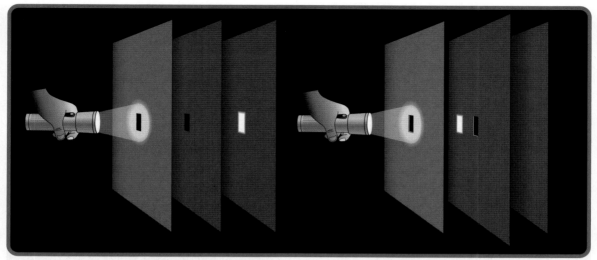

▲ *Do you want to prove that light travels in a straight line? Make a hole at the center of each of two cardboard sheets. (The holes must be the same size.) Line up the holes and shine a flashlight through the first hole. The light will shine through the second hole, too. Move the sheets so that the holes do not line up. What happens?*

through it without scattering them. Tracing paper lets some light pass through, but the paper is not see-through. It is **translucent**. A brick wall or a wooden door is **opaque**—it blocks light rays.

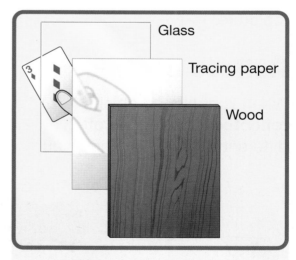

Glass

Tracing paper

Wood

▲ *Glass is transparent, so light passes through easily. (You can see the playing card clearly.) Tracing paper is translucent, letting some light through. No light gets through wood—it is opaque.*

Solar Energy

Even at a distance of 93 million miles (150 million km) from Earth, the Sun is extremely bright. The Sun uses the energy stored in atoms to produce light and heat. That energy speeds across space as **radiation**. Light that is given off by the Sun takes about eight minutes to reach Earth.

Now You See It

People use their eyes all the time—to read, work, watch movies, and play games. More information enters the human brain through the eye than through any other sense organ.

How Do You See?

Light enters the transparent front of the eye, called the **cornea**. A lens **focuses** the light onto the **retina**, a thin layer of tissue that acts like a screen. Light-sensitive cells send nerve signals from the retina to the brain. You "see" a picture.

Reflect on This

When light hits an object, it is **reflected**, or bounced off in a different direction. A chair, your

History in Focus

The ancient Greeks studied the eye 2,500 years ago. Later, Arab scientists discovered that vision had to do with light and the way it bends. During the Middle Ages (about A.D. 400 to 1500), scientists in the Middle East and Europe experimented with lenses to magnify objects, or make them look bigger. The English scientist Roger Bacon (1214–1292) wrote the first description of eyeglasses in 1268.

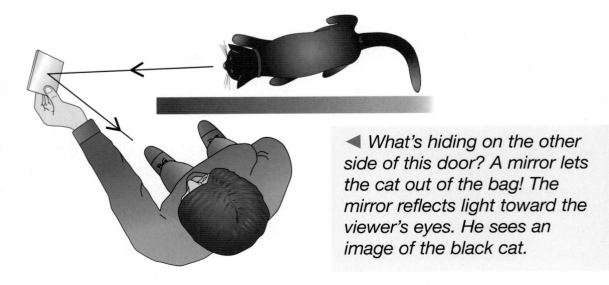

◀ *What's hiding on the other side of this door? A mirror lets the cat out of the bag! The mirror reflects light toward the viewer's eyes. He sees an image of the black cat.*

hand, this book—each of them reflects light. If the light from an object reaches your eyes, you see an **image**. For people who need them, glasses make the image clearer.

▼ *The curved glass of a fun house mirror creates stretched, crunched, and twisted images. The curved glass scatters light, making viewers look taller, wider, or just plain odd!*

Mirror, Mirror

Thousands of years ago, people discovered that a smooth, shiny surface (such as polished metal) reflects light. It acts as a mirror. Light travels in straight lines and bounces off mirrors at the same angle it hits them. A surface that is not perfectly smooth (such as a piece of paper) scatters light rays in different directions.

Eye of the Beholder

The eye is a ball of fluid. Its transparent front, the cornea, lets in light. The **iris** is the colored area of the eye. At the center of the iris, the **pupil** widens or narrows to let in more or less light.

Inside Your Eye

Inside the eye is a small, flexible lens. When light enters the eye, tiny muscles move the lens to adjust the focus. The lens focuses an image on the retina. The image on the retina is upside down because of the way the light rays are bent.

From Eye to Brain

The retina changes the image into nerve signals. Those signals speed along the **optic nerve** to the brain. The brain changes the signals into a picture, right side up. The entire process happens in a flash. Images are updated almost instantly by the eyes and the brain.

▼ *Light is reflected off an object (the pear). The light enters the eye and forms an upside-down image at the back of the eye.*

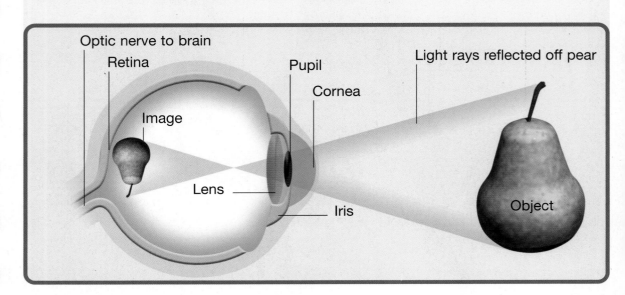

Optic nerve to brain

Retina

Image

Lens

Pupil

Cornea

Iris

Light rays reflected off pear

Object

In Focus

Muscles in the front of the eye change the shape of the lens. These muscles adjust the lens to help you see objects at different distances. Light rays reflected by a faraway object are bent slightly toward one another by the lens. Light rays from an object close to the eye must be bent more to focus the image.

Failure to focus is a common vision problem. Glasses and contact lenses help the eyes' lenses focus properly.

Are Two Eyes Better Than One?

Humans and some other animals have two forward-facing eyes. Their eyes produce **binocular** vision. Because of its position, each eye creates a slightly different image of the same object. The two separate images are combined by the brain. This helps when judging distance. So in animals, two eyes are better than one for climbing, jumping, and hunting.

▼ *Owls have very large, forward-facing eyes. Like people, owls have binocular vision. When hunting, an owl sees a mouse with both eyes at the same time. When the owl's brain turns the two images into a single picture, the bird can judge its distance from the mouse.*

Near and Far

Most young people's eyes are able to make clear images without help. As people get older, many of them need glasses to help their eyes focus properly.

Nearsightedness and Farsightedness

Two common vision problems are **nearsightedness** (myopia) and **farsightedness** (hyperopia). A nearsighted person can see nearby objects clearly. Distant objects look blurry, though. A farsighted person sees distant objects clearly but may be unable to read small print in a book.

Many people experience **presbyopia** by the time they reach the age of 40 or 50. With age, the lens of the eye becomes less flexible. It cannot adjust easily to focus images of nearby objects. Adults sometimes need glasses for reading, sewing, or computer use.

In Living Color

The retina contains two types of light-sensitive cells called **rods**

▼ *If a person is nearsighted, light rays entering the eye focus in front of the retina. If a person is farsighted, the rays focus beyond the retina. The place where the rays meet is called the **focal point**.*

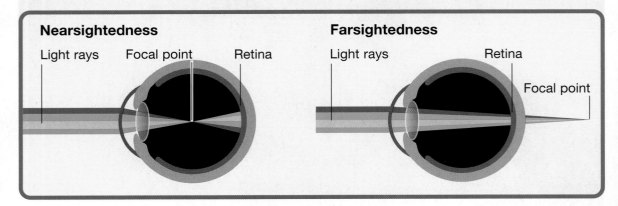

Nearsightedness
Light rays   Focal point   Retina

Farsightedness
Light rays   Retina   Focal point

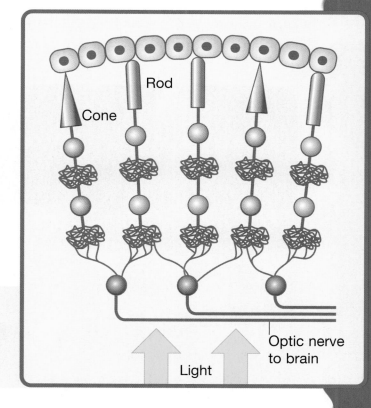

Seeing in the Dark

Ordinary glasses won't help you see in the dark. Members of the military sometimes use a night-vision device. This electronic device has a tube that collects light and intensifies, or boosts, it. The result: The user sees a near-daylight picture.

▲ *This photo of U.S. soldiers making a parachute jump at night was taken using a night-vision device.*

and **cones**. Rods are more sensitive to light but are not good for seeing color. Rods tell the form or shape of an object, even in dim light. Cones are more sensitive to color but less sensitive to light. Cones work only in bright light.

Rod

Cone

Optic nerve to brain

Light

► *The retina contains light-sensitive rods and cones. These cells send messages to the brain through the optic nerve.*

Light and Lenses

In eyeglasses, the lenses do the work by bending light rays. Telescopes, cameras, microscopes, and magnifying glasses also have lenses. They use the same basic idea of bending light.

Bending Light

Light bends naturally when it passes from one material to another—for example, from air through glass or water. You can see this happen by looking into clear water in a shallow pond or a fish tank. Use a stick to poke a stone at the bottom. You will probably miss on your first try! The stone isn't exactly where it appears to be. The stick seems to bend at the point where it enters the water. As light rays pass from air to water, they bend. The bending of light is called **refraction**.

▼ *The lens of a magnifying glass makes objects look bigger. The lens can also distort the image slightly.*

◀ *This diagram shows how light can play tricks on the eye. The pencil seems to bend at the point where it enters the water.*

How a Lens Works

In a **single-focus lens**, all light rays passing through the lens meet at one point—the focal point. A lens can make objects look bigger or smaller. An eye care specialist decides the correct shape and strength of lens a person needs to focus properly. The most common kinds of lenses in eyeglasses are **convex** lenses and **concave** lenses.

A Lens for All Reasons

Lenses have many uses. The lenses in an **optical** microscope can magnify objects up to 2,000 times. Lenses in telescopes and binoculars help people see things that are far away. Lenses are even used in DVD players. A type of light shines onto a disc. The lens helps focus the light so that the player can read the disc.

▶ *The British scientist Robert Hooke (1635–1703) made this early microscope in about 1670. An oil lamp (at the left) provided light. The light was directed through a lens toward the objects he viewed.*

Convex or Concave?

Most lenses in eyeglasses are either convex or concave, on one side or both. The lenses are made of glass or plastic. Plastic is lighter than glass but scratches more easily. Lenses made of **polycarbonate**, a type of tough plastic, are hard to break.

Convex Lenses

A convex lens is thicker in the middle than at the edges. This shape bends light inward, making an image that appears bigger. People who are farsighted wear glasses with convex lenses. The lenses magnify objects that are close to the eyes, such as the printed words in a book. Convex lenses are commonly used in reading glasses.

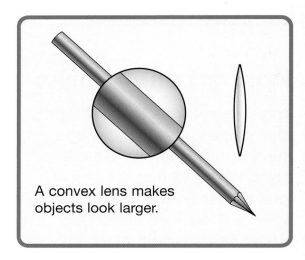

A convex lens makes objects look larger.

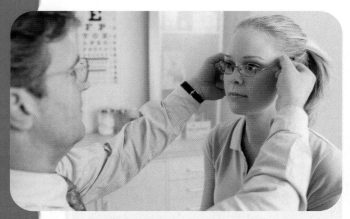

▲ *An eye care specialist makes sure glasses correct vision properly and fit comfortably.*

On Fire

Convex lenses bend light rays toward one another. A convex lens can set fire to a piece of paper by concentrating the light (and heat) of the Sun at the lens's focal point. Did you know discarded glass bottles sometimes start forest fires? The glass acts as a lens, concentrating the Sun's rays and setting dry leaves on fire. So don't litter. Recycle instead!

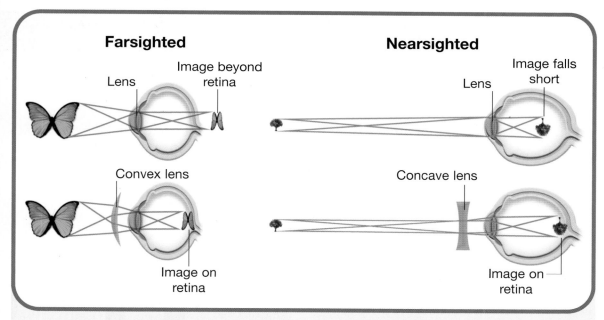

Farsighted

Lens

Image beyond retina

Convex lens

Image on retina

Nearsighted

Lens

Image falls short

Concave lens

Image on retina

▲ *A farsighted person has trouble seeing objects that are close. The eye focuses most objects beyond the retina. A convex lens can correct this problem. A nearsighted person has trouble seeing objects in the distance. The eye focuses most objects short of the retina. A concave lens can correct nearsightedness.*

Concave Lenses

A concave lens makes an image that looks smaller. This type of lens is thinner in the middle than at the edges. It bends light outward. People who are nearsighted can wear glasses with concave lenses to correct their vision. The lens gives a clearer image of distant objects, making them look less blurred.

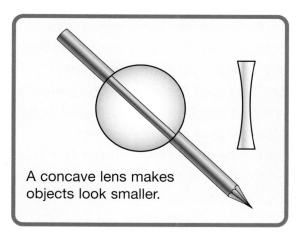

A concave lens makes objects look smaller.

Charting Your Vision

Today, many people have their eyes and vision checked regularly. In the past, people with vision problems could get little medical help. Doctors did not clearly understand the eye and the process of seeing.

Early Eyeglasses

The first glasses were invented in Italy in about 1285. They were held in the hand or stuck on the nose. Spectacles, or glasses with temple frames, came into use during the 1700s. By then, eye doctors knew to prescribe lenses of different strengths to correct people's vision problems.

Eye Exams

What kinds of doctors carry out complete eye exams? **Ophthalmologists** are medical doctors who specialize in eye care. They prescribe eyeglasses and contact lenses. They also perform eye surgery and treat medical problems of the eye. **Optometrists** are eye doctors who can prescribe glasses and contact lenses and treat eye diseases with medicines. Some optometrists perform certain minor surgeries.

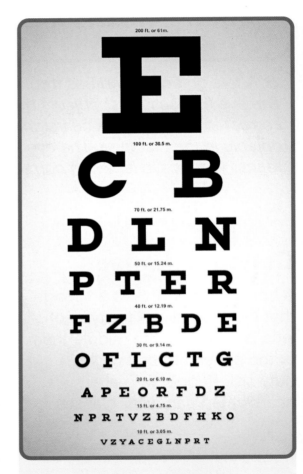

▲ *Can you see* E *now? A vision-testing chart has the biggest letters at the top. The letters on the lower lines are smaller.*

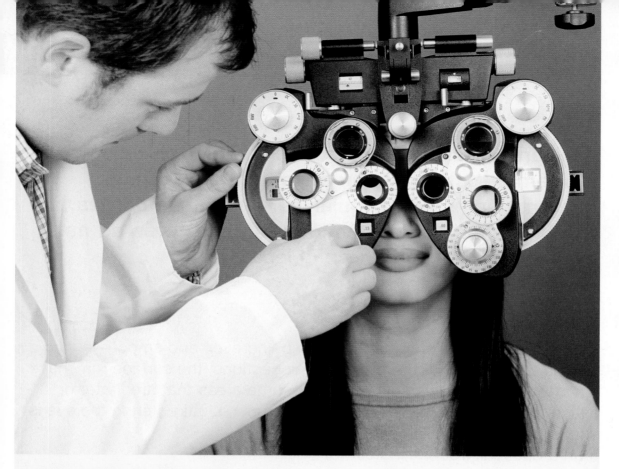

▲ *An eye doctor checks a patient's vision with a **phoropter**. The doctor adjusts this device to decide the type and strength of lenses the patient needs.*

During an eye exam, a person reads lines of letters on a chart. Distance vision (for driving and watching TV), near vision (for reading), and intermediate vision (for computer use) are checked. The doctor examines the eyes to make sure that they work together properly. Machines test how well the eyes focus. A person's **field of vision** (the area each eye sees) is also tested.

Tools of the Trade

Eye doctors have special tests and tools to check for vision problems. The doctor uses an **ophthalmoscope** to look at the parts at the front of and inside each eye. He or she may put drops in the eye to make the pupils bigger. That gives a better view of the inside of the eye. The doctor also checks for infection or disease.

A New View

Regular eye tests can help spot common vision problems, such as **astigmatism** and **strabismus**. Astigmatism is an irregular curving of the cornea. Strabismus is a condition in which both eyes do not align when focusing on an object.

Out of Focus

Astigmatism happens when the cornea, at the front of the eye, is distorted. A person with an astigmatism usually has a cornea shaped more like a football (oval) than a baseball (round). Instead of being even and smooth in all directions, the surface may have some areas that are flatter or steeper. Light entering the eye is

▼ *During an eye examination, a doctor uses a machine to look closely at the outside and the inside of the eye.*

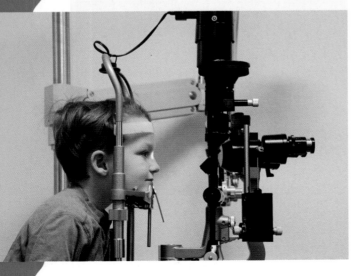

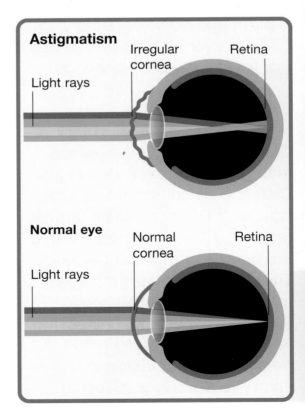

Astigmatism
Light rays
Irregular cornea
Retina

Normal eye
Light rays
Normal cornea
Retina

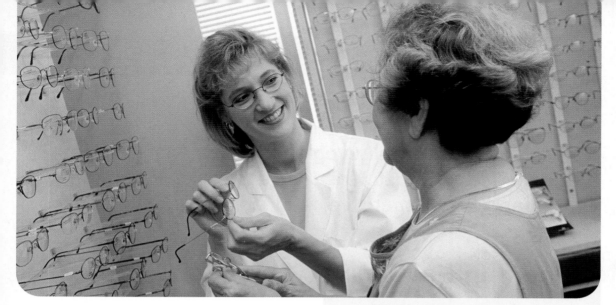

▲ Eyeglasses have changed a lot since they were invented hundreds of years ago. People can choose from a wide variety of styles and materials.

not focused properly to a single point. The image that is produced is out of focus. Astigmatism is corrected by wearing glasses or contact lenses that focus light on one spot on the retina. The result is a clear image.

What Is Strabismus?

In a person with strabismus, the eyes look in different directions. They do not focus at the same time on a single point. One or both of the eyes may turn in, out,

◄ In astigmatism, the light rays from an object do not meet at one point. Blurred vision occurs. It can be corrected with glasses or contact lenses.

up, or down. Strabismus is sometimes called wandering eye or crossed eyes.

Strabismus is a common eye problem in children. It can sometimes be treated with exercises, eyedrops, or an eye patch. Those treatments help make the eye muscles stronger. Doctors may also prescribe glasses with special lenses called **prisms**. Prisms can help align images in certain cases. Some children need an operation to correct strabismus.

Making a Spectacle

Before the 1900s, all eyeglass lenses were made of glass. Today, most lenses are plastic. Plastic is lighter and less expensive, and it breaks less easily than glass.

Framed in Fashion

Early eyeglasses were usually clipped to the bridge of the nose. The pince-nez (French for "pinch nose") had frames made of bone, metal, wood, or leather. Today, most frames are made of plastic or strong, lightweight metals. The temples have a wire core inside them for strength.

Lens Looks

Some lenses have a special coating to protect them from being scratched. Lenses can also be tinted a color. Tinted lenses filter out some light rays. High-index lenses are made of a special plastic that bends light differently than regular plastic lenses do. High-index lenses can correct vision with less material, so the lenses are thinner and lighter.

What Are Bifocals?

Bifocal lenses have two sections of different strengths. Some people need two different prescriptions — one for distance and another for

◄ *Pince-nez glasses were popular in the mid-1800s. These glasses clipped onto the nose.*

reading, for example. With bifocals, they need only one pair of glasses. Trifocals are similar but have three sections with different strengths. Progressive lenses change strength gradually from top to bottom. Unlike bifocals and trifocals, progressive lenses have no dividing lines as the focus changes.

Birth of Bifocals

In 1784, American politician and scientist Benjamin Franklin (1706–1790) invented bifocals. He called them "double spectacles." Franklin was tired of wearing two pairs of glasses, one for reading and the other for distance. He cut the lenses in half from side to side. Then he placed the two half-lenses together in a frame. He used the upper half for viewing distant objects. The lower half of the lenses was for reading.

▲ Modern frames are very different from the early pince-nez! Today, eyeglass wearers have many choices of styles and materials.

▼ This statue of Benjamin Franklin shows him wearing bifocal glasses. He invented them in 1784.

A Look at Contacts

Some people choose to wear contact lenses instead of glasses. These tiny, thin plastic lenses are placed directly on the surface of the eye. They float on a layer of tears.

What Are Contact Lenses?

Contact lenses are small, thin, curved plastic disks that cover the cornea. They correct the same vision problems that eyeglasses correct. Several types of lenses are available for people with different needs. An eye doctor must provide a prescription. When used with care, contact lenses are a safe way to correct vision.

Why Wear Contacts?

People choose to wear contact lenses for different reasons. Some people prefer how they look without glasses. Many athletes like the comfort and convenience. Eyeglasses can steam up or be knocked off. Contacts also give a wider range of vision.

▼ *It is important to wash your hands before handling contact lenses.*

▲ Rap and hip-hop star and actor Coolio wore colored contact lenses (and fangs) for a scary effect at a music awards ceremony.

Lenses Over Time

The Italian inventor, artist, and scientist Leonardo da Vinci (1452–1519) sketched his design for contact lenses in 1508! More than 300 years later, the idea finally became a reality. A Swiss eye doctor made the first contact lenses in about 1887. His contacts were uncomfortable. They were made of glass and covered the entire front surface of the eye.

In the 1930s, people began to make contact lenses from plastic. The lenses were molded to fit the eye. They had to be taken out frequently, though, because they blocked the natural flow of tears. By 1950, smaller contact lenses covered only the cornea.

Modern contact lenses are made of flexible plastic that lets oxygen reach the eye to keep the cornea healthy. Some people with astigmatism can correct their vision with **toric contact lenses**. There are even bifocal contact lenses.

Types of Contacts

In the 1950s, all contact lenses were made of hard plastic. Soft contacts were introduced in the 1970s. They are more flexible. Many people find soft contacts more comfortable to wear. Many soft contact lenses are disposable. They are designed to be thrown away after a short period of use. Some extended-wear lenses can be worn for up to a month without being removed.

Protect Your Eyes

Some people wear sunglasses for fashion—even when it's cloudy! Sunglasses have a useful purpose, though. They protect the eyes from bright sunlight or reflected glare that could be harmful.

Sun Safety

Sunglasses with tinted lenses screen out some rays of visible light. The color of the tint decides the parts of the **light spectrum** that are absorbed. The rays people cannot see, however, can cause the most eye damage. It is important to wear sunglasses that block out the Sun's invisible **ultraviolet (UV) radiation**. Lenses with UV coating absorb harmful UV rays.

▼ *Sunglasses are more than fashion statements. They are important for good eye health.*

Lenses that darken automatically when exposed to sunlight are called **photochromic**. A chemical reaction to UV rays in sunlight makes the lenses absorb parts of the visible light spectrum. Indoors, the lenses work just like those in ordinary glasses.

Glare Grabbers

How are polarized sunglasses different from ordinary sunglasses? Polarized sunglasses don't just block light. They also reduce glare. Normal light vibrates in all directions. **Polarized light** vibrates in one

▼ *Polarized lenses filter out some of the rays in sunlight to reduce glare.*

▲ *Scientists wear protective safety glasses when handling chemicals in laboratories.*

direction. Light reflected from surfaces such as a flat road or smooth water is usually polarized horizontally. In polarized lenses, a filter blocks horizontal light rays.

Mirrored sunglasses also block glare. The lenses have a special coating that reflects sunlight away from the eye, to reduce glare.

Playing It Safe

Safety glasses will not shatter if hit by a flying object or a hot spark. They protect eyes from harmful liquids and dust. Many people, such as surgeons and electricians, wear eye protection on the job.

Extreme Visors

Wraparound safety glasses are effective because they provide protection at the front and the sides of the eyes. Racing drivers and astronauts wear protective visors that completely cover their faces. The visors shield their eyes from heat, chemicals, or impact. Astronauts need protection from the blinding sunlight in space.

▶ *An astronaut wears a reflective visor for protection from glaring sunlight in space.*

27

Seeing Is Believing

Modern life has put new demands on the human eye. It has also brought advances in eye care that will help people see the future clearly.

From Stone Age to Digital Age

Prehistoric people used their eyes mainly for hunting and finding food. Today, many people use their eyes for hours while working on computers or watching TV. These close-range activities can strain the eyes. A person who sits in front of a screen all day uses his or her eyes very differently from a Stone Age hunter!

Eye on the Future

The digital age has also brought improvements in eye care. With the latest tools and tests, doctors can more quickly and easily identify vision problems. New drugs can

▼ *Take good care of your eyes! They should last you a lifetime.*

Get the Facts

- About 64 percent of American adults wear eyeglasses, according to VisionWatch.
- The jobs people most associate with wearing glasses are librarian, teacher, and lawyer.
- More than 70 percent of sports-related eye injuries happen to people under age 25. Protective eyewear could prevent 90 percent of those injuries.
- Does your spaniel need shades? Some companies sell sunglasses for dogs!

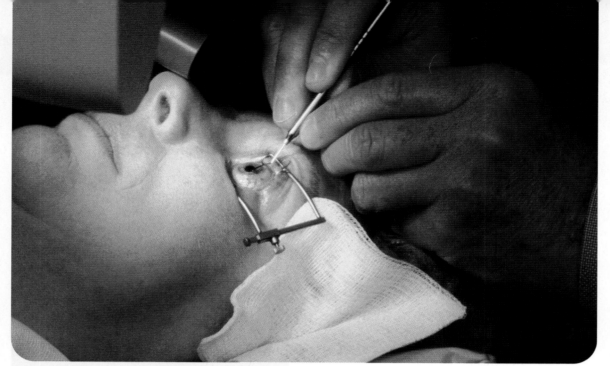

▲ *Advances in surgery have increased patients' options and improved vision.*

help treat certain eye diseases and prevent loss of sight.

Cutting-edge operations are helping people see more clearly. In the past decade, millions have had **laser** eye surgery. A surgeon cuts a flap in the surface of the cornea. The doctor then uses a laser to reshape the cornea so that light focuses properly on the retina. Surgeons also **transplant** healthy corneas from donors to replace damaged or diseased corneas.

What advances might you see as you look to the future? Some researchers say a bionic eye that will reverse blindness could be available within a few years.

Laser Eye Surgery

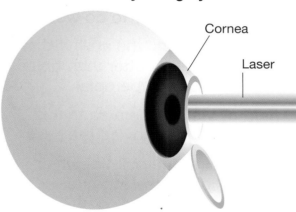

Cornea

Laser

▲ *Lasers are a special form of light. In laser surgery, the surgeon uses a laser or a thin blade to cut a flap in the cornea. A laser then removes some tissue from the inner part of the cornea. The reshaped cornea focuses images clearly on the retina.*

Glossary

astigmatism: irregular curve of the cornea

atoms: tiny particles that make up all matter

bifocal: having lenses with two different strengths

binocular: with both eyes

concave: curved inward

cones: cells in the retina that enable color vision

convex: curved outward

cornea: the clear, outer covering of the eye

energy: the ability to do work

farsightedness: the ability to see distant objects better than objects that are close (hyperopia)

field of vision: the area that is visible without moving the eyes

focal point: the point at which rays of light come together

focuses: brings together at one point

glare: harshly bright light

image: a picture of an object formed by a mirror or a lens

iris: the colored part of the eye

laser: a narrow, strong beam of light

lenses: glass or other clear material curved to make light rays move together or apart; the curved, clear parts of the eyes that focus light on the retina

light spectrum: the range of colors in visible light

nearsightedness: the ability to see close objects better than objects that are far away (myopia)

opaque: not letting light through

ophthalmologists: doctors who specialize in diseases of the eye

ophthalmoscope: an instrument for viewing the inside of the eye

optical: having to do with the eye

optic nerve: the nerve that carries signals from the retina to the brain

optometrists: doctors who prescribe glasses and contact lenses and treat eye diseases with medicines

phoropter: an instrument used to determine a person's corrective lens prescription

photochromic: able to change color when exposed to sunlight

photons: tiny particles of light

polarized light: light that vibrates in only one direction

polycarbonate: a strong plastic

presbyopia: decreased ability to change focus between distant and near objects

prescription: a written order for corrective lenses or medicine

prisms: lenses that can separate white light into colors

pupil: the opening in the center of the eye through which light enters

radiation: energy in the form of waves or tiny particles

rays: beams of light or other energy

reflected: bounced back after hitting a surface

refraction: the bending of light as it passes from one material to another

retina: the lining at the back of the eyeball that receives images

rods: light-sensitive cells in the retina

single-focus lens: a lens that cannot change shape to bring objects at different distances into focus

strabismus: a condition in which both eyes do not align when focusing on an object

toric contact lenses: lenses used to correct astigmatism

translucent: allowing some light to pass through

transparent: allowing all light to pass through

transplant: to transfer an organ from one person to another

ultraviolet (UV) radiation: invisible light from the Sun that can harm unprotected eyes

Find Out More

Discovery Channel: Human Body Explorer—Sight
dsc.discovery.com/tv/human-body/explorer/explorer.html
Take an interactive journey through the wonders of sight.

Optical Society of America: Exploring the Science of Light
www.opticsforkids.org/futurescientists/intermediate
Future scientists will enjoy these experiments that teach about properties of light.

Publisher's note to educators and parents: Our editors have carefully reviewed these web sites to ensure that they are suitable for children. Many web sites change frequently, however, and we cannot guarantee that a site's future contents will continue to meet our high standards of quality and educational value. Be advised that children should be closely supervised whenever they access the Internet.

Index